Table of Contents

Romantic Recipes for Lovers

Recipes to Spice Up Your Love Life!!

BY: Ida Smith

License Notes

Introduction

Do you have a planned romantic evening with your partner and you are at a crossroad on what meals and drinks to prepare for this evening?

Panic no more; there are more than enough foods and drinks recipe for you and your partner to try out in this recipe book.

When we say that we have your love life under culinary control, trust us that we do!!

Pork chops

This is for the lovers of pork!!!

Preparation Time: 05 Minutes
Cooking Time: 15 Minutes
Yield: 2
Ingredient List:

- 1 teaspoon canola oil
- 1 pinch pepper
- 1 pinch salt
- 1 tablespoon Italian seasoning
- 2 pork chops

Preparation:

Preheat the skillet to 356 degrees F.

Marinate the pork in a bowl of seasoning, pepper, and salt.

Place the pork in the skillet of oil, sear till both sides are browned.

Serve.

Flame of Love

It is burning up in here!!! Could it be love sparks flying??!!!

Preparation Time: 04 Minutes
Cooking Time: Nil
Yield: 2
Ingredient List:

- 6 flamed grapefruit twists
- 1 oz. dry sherry
- 4 oz. Monkey 47

Preparation:

Pour the Monkey 47 and sherry in a mixing glass.

Mix well.

Serve in the glasses and garnish with the flamed twists.

Cauliflower Gnocchi

Little awesome nuggets of deliciousness!!!

Preparation Time: 10 Minutes
Cooking Time: 15 Minutes
Yield: 2
Ingredient List:

- 1 pinch salt
- 8 ounces cauliflower florets
- 1 cup soy sauce
- 6 tablespoons flour

Preparation:
Cook the cauliflower in a pot of water.
Cook for 4 minutes.
Spread out the cooked cauliflower on a paper towel.

Drain out all the water from the cauliflower.

Put the cauliflower, salt, and flour in a processor.

Process till you get a sticky and soft dough.

Put the dough on a floured surface.

Then cut out the dough into 3 sections, and roll each of the sections to make ropes.

Then cut out the ropes into pieces.

Fry the gnocchi pieces in a pan of oil.

Turn off the heat and pour the sauce into the pan.

Mix with the gnocchi.

Serve with a sprinkle of the desired herbs.

Enjoy.

Edinburgh Rose

Where this cocktail is, love lives there!!

Preparation Time: 04 Minutes
Cooking Time: Nil
Yield: 2
Ingredient List:

- 6 raspberries
- 30ml organic raspberry
- 2 oz. rose cordial champagne
- 40ml gin (Hendricks)
- 40ml lychee juice

Preparation:

Combine the liquid ingredients in a shaker.
Shake well.
Toss in the raspberries.
Enjoy.

Shrimp Fried Rice

In less than 30 minutes, this meal is ready for your devouring!!!

Preparation Time: 10 Minutes

Cooking Time: 25 Minutes

Yield: 2

Ingredient List:

- 1 pinch black pepper
- 1 pinch salt
- 1 pound deveined, peeled shrimps (raw)
- 2 beaten medium eggs
- 2 tablespoons canola oil
- 3 cups cooked white rice
- 1 teaspoon cornstarch
- 1 large handful sliced green onion
- 1 tablespoon sesame oil

- 1 tablespoon coconut aminos
- 8 oz. peas and carrot (diced carrots)

Preparation:
Combine the black pepper, salt, cornstarch, and shrimps in a bowl, keep aside to marinate.
Pour the canola oil in a pan. Throw in the shrimps.
Transfer to a bowl when the shrimps are ready.
In the same pan, fry the egg for 2 minutes and transfer to another bowl too.
Pour another oil into the pan, add the green onion.
Cook for 3 minutes.
Add in the cooked rice, stir-cook for 2 minutes.
Stir in the coconut aminos, carrots, peas, and sesame oil.
Stir-cook for 3 minutes before adding the shrimps and egg.
Cook for 2 minutes.
Serve and enjoy.

Creamy Chicken and Rice

If chicken and rice are the favorite meal of any of you, then you both will enjoy this salivating and creamy version of the meal!!

Preparation Time: 05 Minutes
Cooking Time: 15 Minutes
Yield: 2
Ingredient List:

- – 1 pinch salt
- – 1 tablespoon butter
- – 2 handfuls white rice
- – 1 diced yellow onion
- – 1 chunked chicken breast
- – 1 pinch garlic powder
- – 8 tablespoons shredded cheddar cheese

- 1 pinch dried thyme
- 6 tablespoons sour cream
- 4 ounces mixed vegetables
- 1 cup chicken broth

Preparation:
Put butter in a pin. Sauté the onion for 2 minutes.
Throw in the chicken. Cook for 4 minutes.
Add in the garlic powder, rice, broth, thyme, and salt.
Cook and allow simmering.
Throw in the vegetables, cook for additional 3 minutes.
Stir in the cheese and sour cream.
Cook for another 2 minutes to allow melting.
Serve and enjoy.

Starry Sonata

There is no better way to end the evening than to watch the stars as you sip this cocktail.

Preparation Time: 04 Minutes
Cooking Time: Nil
Yield: 2
Ingredient List:

- 2 star anises
- 1 oz. sherry
- 3 parts Drambuie
- 4 dashes Angostura bitters
- 1 oz. bourbon

Preparation:

Throw in the second to the last ingredients into mixing glass with ice cubes.
Mix well before straining into two glasses.
Garnish each glass with star anise.

Love Potion

Well, the name speaks for itself!!!

Preparation Time: 03 Minutes
Cooking Time: Nil
Yield: 2
Ingredient List:

- 4 oz. rose champagne
- 1 oz. lemon juice
- 1 oz. elderflower liquor
- 3 oz. gin

Preparation:
Combine the liquor, gin, and lemon juice into a shaker.

Shake well and strain into a glass of ice.
Add the rose champagne as a topping.
Garnish with rose petals.

The Smoke Show

Intriguing!!!

Preparation Time: 04 Minutes
Cooking Time: Nil
Yield: 2
Ingredient List:

- 1 oz. agave nectar
- 1 oz. tequila
- 2 oz. Casamigos Mezcal
- 2 oz. lemon juice
- 1 pinch sugar
- 1 pinch salt
- 1 pinch Tajin

– 1 oz. Ancho Reyes

Preparation:
Rim your glasses with a mix of Tajin, sugar, and salt.
Throw the remaining ingredients into a shaker.
Add a handful of ice cubes. Shake well.
Strain into the glasses.

Seared Salmon and Apple Sauce

Exotic and sophisticated!!!

Preparation Time: 05 Minutes
Cooking Time: 15 Minutes
Yield: 2
Ingredient List:

- 1 pinch nutmeg
- 1 teaspoon olive oil
- 1 pinch ginger powder
- 10 tablespoons applesauce
- 3 skinned salmon fillets
- 1 teaspoon salt
- 1 tablespoon pepper

– 1 pinch garlic

Preparation:
Preheat your oven to 352 degrees F.
Coat the baking dish with a little portion of oil.
Throw in the nutmeg, ginger, garlic, and applesauce in a pot.
Stir well and cook for 2 minutes.
Season the salmon in a bowl of pepper and salt first.
Then, coat the fillet in the applesauce mixture.
Arrange the fillet in the prepared baking dish.
Roast for 15 minutes.
Serve with the remaining applesauce.

Spicy Pumpkin Seeds

Something appetizing to snack on before it's meal o'clock!!!

Preparation Time: 05 Minutes

Cooking Time: 15 Minutes

Yield: 2

Ingredient List:

- 1 tablespoon canola oil
- 2 handfuls dry pumpkin seeds
- 1 pinch cayenne powder
- 1 pinch salt
- 1 pinch garlic powder

Preparation:

Preheat the oven to 374 degrees F.

Toss in the ingredients into a medium bowl. Mix well.

Pour the mixture on a baking sheet. Spread them out.

Bake till the seeds are toasted.

Serve and enjoy.

Love Struck

Do you want your partner to get high in love with you? Then, a sip of this cocktail is all you need!!

Preparation Time: 04 Minutes

Cooking Time: Nil

Yield: 2

Ingredient List:

- 2 oz. syrup
- 4 oz. vodka
- 2 oz. cranberry juice
- 1 oz. La Marca Prosecco
- 1 oz. lemon juice
- 4 oz. fruit liqueur

Preparation:
Throw in all your ingredients in a shaker, except the Prosecco.
Shake well.
Strain into two glasses.
Top with the Prosecco. Enjoy.

French Onion Soup

Travel to French with your loved one by making this recipe!!!!

Preparation Time: 10 Minutes

Cooking Time: 40 Minutes

Yield: 2

Ingredient List:

- 1 tablespoon oil
- 4 tablespoons butter
- 1 pinch salt
- 1 pinch pepper
- 1 cup sliced onion
- 1 pinch dried thyme
- 1 tablespoon dry sherry
- 1 can beef broth

- 2 slices French bread
- 2 slices provolone cheese
- 2 tablespoons grated parmesan cheese
- 1 diced slice Swiss cheese

Preparation:
Preheat your oven broiler.
Sauté the onions in a pan of melted butter and oil.
Throw in the thyme, sherry, pepper, salt, and broth.
Cook and allow simmering for 20 minutes.
Scoop the mixture into bowls.
Top each bowl with a slice of bread and each of the cheeses.
Heat the bowls in the oven until the cheeses brown slightly and become bubbly.
Enjoy.

Mushroom Stroganoff

A mushroom meal can be romantic too!!!

Preparation Time: 05 Minutes
Cooking Time: 15 Minutes
Yield: 2
Ingredient List:

- 200g cooked wild rice
- 250g chopped mushrooms (mixed)
- 2 tablespoons canola oil
- 1 crushed garlic
- 1 chopped medium onion
- 1 tablespoon paprika
- 1 cup broth
- 1 handful chopped parsley

- 4 tablespoons sour cream
- 1 tablespoon Worcestershire sauce

Preparation:
Sauté the onion in a pan of oil.
Throw in the paprika and garlic.
Cook for 2 minutes before adding the mushrooms.
Turn off the heat and stir in the parsley and sour cream. Stir well.
Serve the mixture with wild rice.

Cupid's Champagne

If you are looking for a perfect drink for your lover, here it is!!!

Preparation Time: 04 Minutes
Cooking Time: Nil
Yield: 2
Ingredient List:

- 2 ounces vodka
- 2-part champagne
- 2 ounces peach puree

Preparation:
Put the puree and vodka in a shaker of ice.
Shake well.

Strain into two glasses.
Top each glass with champagne.

What/When

The name is not the only thrilling thing about this drink, the taste is exceptionally amazing too!!

Preparation Time: 03 Minutes

Cooking Time: Nil

Yield: 2

Ingredient List:

- 4 oz. Prosecco
- 1 oz. syrup
- 1 oz. blood orange puree
- 4 oz. The Botanist Gin
- 1 oz. lemon juice

Preparation:

Combine your ingredients in a mixer.
Mix well.
Serve into your glasses.

Lemon Chicken

This has to be our favorite chicken recipe for lovers!!!

Preparation Time: 05 Minutes
Cooking Time: 30 Minutes
Yield: 2
Ingredient List:

- 3 tablespoons lemon juice
- 2 pounds chicken parts (cut into pieces)
- 1 crushed garlic clove
- 2 tablespoons lemon zest
- 1 tablespoon chopped thyme
- 1 pinch black pepper
- 1 pinch salt

- 1 tablespoon soft butter
- 1 teaspoon chopped rosemary

Preparation:
Preheat the oven to 424 degrees F.
Place the chicken, lemon zest, lemon juice, salt, thyme, garlic, rosemary, and pepper in a bowl.
Allow marinating for 35 minutes.
Place the chicken pieces in a baking dish.
Brush the chicken with butter and pour the marinade juice over it.
Bake for 30 minutes till they are crispy brown.
Serve the chicken with juice.

Chicken Parmesan

Crispy and delicious doesn't start to describe this meal because this meal is phenomenal!!!

Preparation Time: 05 Minutes

Cooking Time: 15 Minutes

Yield: 2

Ingredient List:

- 1 egg
- 2 halves, skinless chicken breasts (boneless)
- 2 tablespoons oil
- 4 tablespoons flour
- 5 tablespoons panko breadcrumbs
- 4 tablespoons grated Parmesan cheese
- 1 tablespoon parsley

- 5 tablespoons Italian seasoning breadcrumbs
- 12 ounces marinara sauce
- 2 tablespoons shredded Parmesan cheese
- 8 tablespoons shredded mozzarella cheese

Preparation:
Preheat the oven to 426 degrees F.
Break the egg in a bowl. Whisk well.
Put the flour in another bowl.
Mix the breadcrumbs, parsley, pepper, salt, and grated Parmesan cheese in another bowl.
Coat the chicken in the bowl of flour first, and then in the egg bowl.
And further in the breadcrumbs mixture bowl.
Fry the chicken in a pan of oil for 5 minutes.
Pour the sauce into a baking dish.
Throw in the fried chicken pieces.
Top with shredded cheeses.
Bake for 15 minutes.
Serve with rice.

Blushing Rosemary

Something nice to make the beautiful lady blush all evening!!!

Preparation Time: 03 Minutes
Cooking Time: Nil
Yield: 2
Ingredient List:

- 4 dashes lemon bitters
- 8 parts agave nectar
- 4 parts tequila
- 2 rosemary sprigs
- 2-part lemon juice
- 8 watermelon chunks

Preparation:
Muddle the herbs and fruit in a shaker.
Throw in the remaining ingredients.
Mix well.
Serve into two glasses.
Add a garnish of rosemary sprig each.

It is a Match!!

I guarantee that your partner will love this drink!!

Preparation Time: 05 Minutes

Cooking Time: Nil

Yield: 2

Ingredient List:

- 3 crumbled basil leaves
- 4 oz. Ketel One Citroen vodka
- 3 muddled strawberries
- 1 oz. syrup
- 1 dash lemon juice

Preparation:

Mix the ingredients in a mixer.
Add ice cubes. Mix well.
Strain into glasses.
Enjoy.

Royal Romance

Let's make your romantic dinner a grand affair!!!

Preparation Time: 03 Minutes
Cooking Time: Nil
Yield: 2
Ingredient List:

- 2 oz. gin
- 2 dashes grenadine
- 1-part passion fruit juice
- 1-part triple sec

Preparation:
Combine the ingredients and ice cubes into a shaker.

Shake well.
Serve into two glasses.
Enjoy.

Pink Lady

A delicious drink to celebrate your beautiful lady, and you too, of course!!!

Preparation Time: 03 Minutes
Cooking Time: Nil
Yield: 2
Ingredient List:

 – 1 oz. egg white
 – 1 dash lemon juice
 – 3 oz. gin
 – 1 dash grenadine
 – 1 dash apple brandy

Preparation:

Combine the ingredients and ice cubes in a mixer.
Mix well.
Strain into 2 glasses.
Garnish with cherries.

Spaghetti Carbonara

This is the simplest spaghetti recipe you'd ever come across!!!

Preparation Time: 05 Minutes

Cooking Time: 10 Minutes

Yield: 2

Ingredient List:

- 1 tablespoon chopped parsley
- 4 ounces spaghetti (cooked)
- 2 sliced portions of bacon (diced)
- 1 tablespoon salt
- 1 tablespoon black pepper
- 4 tablespoon grated Parmesan
- 1 large egg

– 2 minced clove garlic

Preparation:
Mix the Parmesan and egg in a bowl.
Cook the bacon in a pan for 4 minutes.
Add in the garlic. Cook for 2 minutes.
Throw in the egg mixture, a tablespoon of water, and spaghetti.
Season with pepper and salt.
Serve.

The Honey Bee

Tall glasses of beauty!!!!

Preparation Time: 04 Minutes
Cooking Time: Nil
Yield: 2
Ingredient List:

– 2 dashes of Prosecco
– 6 dashes walnut bitters
– 1 oz. Drambuie

Preparation:
Add the walnut bitters and Drambuie in the two champagne flutes.
Add a dash of prosecco each to the flutes.

Stir.
Garnish with orange wheels.

Avocado Sauce

This sauce is pure bliss!! Let's try it!!

Preparation Time: 03 Minutes
Cooking Time: Nil
Yield: 2
Ingredient List:

- 1 minced large garlic
- 1 pitted, halved large ripe avocado
- 1 pinch cracked black pepper
- 8 tablespoons sour cream
- 2 tablespoons lemon juice
- 1 pinch salt

Preparation:
Combine all the ingredients smoothly.
Serve with chicken.

Lemon Peppered Prawns

This dish is for all the prawn lovers out there!!!

Preparation Time: 04 Minutes
Cooking Time: 05 Minutes
Yield: 2
Ingredient List:

- 1 squeeze lemon juice
- 1 teaspoon garlic powder
- 1 tablespoon flour
- 1 teaspoon salt
- 1 tablespoon butter
- 1 tablespoon canola oil

- 1 pinch black pepper
- 1 pound deveined medium prawns
- 1 teaspoon lemon pepper

Preparation:
Wash and pat the prawns dry.
Mix the salt, garlic, prawns, pepper, flour, and lemon pepper in a bowl.
Mix well.
Add the butter and oil to a pan.
When the mixture is heated, fry the prawns till both sides are done.
A few minutes to when you want to pack them, add a squeeze of lemon juice.
Serve and garnish with lemon slices.

Turkey Piccata

Let try something with turkey, and I guarantee that your lover will definitely love it!!!

Preparation Time: 10 Minutes
Cooking Time: 15 Minutes
Yield: 2
Ingredient List:

- 4 tablespoons dry white wine
- 1 tablespoon butter
- 1 pinch black pepper
- 1 tablespoon chopped shallots
- 4 turkey cutlets
- 1 teaspoon olive oil
- 1 pinch salt
- 3 tablespoons broth
- 1 teaspoon sliced garlic
- 1 pinch flour

- 1 tablespoon chopped parsley
- 1 tablespoon drained capers
- 1 tablespoon lemon juice

Preparation:
Marinate the turkey with pepper and salt. Keep aside.
Sear the turkey in a pan of oil. Cook till done.
Transfer to a paper-lined plate.
Add butter to the pan, and sauté the garlic and shallots.
Throw in the wine, cook for 2 minutes while you scrape the pan.
Toss in the flour and broth.
Cook for 4 minutes to allow the mixture boil up.
Turn off the heat and toss in the juice, sauce, and capers.
Stir well.
Serve with a sprinkle of parsley.

Spicy Love Affair

This drink is scintillating!!!

Preparation Time: 04 Minutes
Cooking Time: Nil
Yield: 2
Ingredient List:

- 3 oz. vodka
- 6 oz. pink grapefruit juice
- 2 oz. ginger syrup.
- 2 dashes lemon juice

Preparation:
Mix the vodka, syrup, and grapefruit juice in a mixer.

Mix well.
Pour into the glasses.
Top each glass with a dash of lemon juice.
Enjoy.

Broccoli and Mushroom

What an amazing culinary combo!!

Preparation Time: 05 Minutes
Cooking Time: 10 Minutes
Yield: 2
Ingredient List:

- 1 teaspoon grapeseed oil
- 1 tablespoon soy sauce
- 1 teaspoon sugar
- 1 tablespoon rice vinegar
- 5 oz. sliced mushrooms
- 1 minced garlic clove
- 1 cup broccoli florets

- 2 tablespoons water
- 1 pinch red pepper flakes
- 1 tablespoon minced ginger

Preparation:
Combine the sugar, sauce, and vinegar in a bowl. Mix well.
Sauté the ginger, pepper flakes, and garlic in a pan of oil.
Cook for 1 minute.
Throw in the water, mushrooms, and broccoli.
Cook for 7 minutes.
Throw in the soy sauce mixture, and stir well.
Serve with a sprinkle of toasted sesame seeds.

Shrimp and Couscous

Satisfactorily delicious!!

Preparation Time: 2o Minutes
Cooking Time: 15 Minutes
Yield: 2
Ingredient List:

- 1 handful peas
- 1 shredded carrot
- 2 handfuls couscous
- 1 pinch mustard seed
- 2 sliced garlic
- 1 sliced leek
- 1 tablespoon canola oil
- 1 pinch coarse salt
- 1 pound shelled, deveined shrimp
- 1 teaspoon pepper

Preparation:

Fry the shrimps in a pan of it.

Season with pepper and salt.

Stir well.

Transfer to a paper-lined bowl.

Throw in the mustard seeds into the pan.

When the seeds start popping, toss in the garlic, carrots, and leeks.

Cook-stir for 3 minutes.

Throw in the peas and couscous.

Add a cup of water.

Season with pepper and salt.

Cook for 6 minutes.

Turn off heat.

Throw in the shrimps.

Mix well.

Serve.

Conclusion

Well!

We have come to the end of this romantic cookbook, and we dare to say that this recipe book is as special as they come, and we can't help but be jealous of you and your partner because this cookbook features amazing recipes that won't only rekindle your love but will whet your appetite.

With all of these recipes, you and your part are in an amazing and memorable evening!!!

Don't miss out!

Visit the website below and you can sign up to receive emails whenever Ida Smith publishes a new book. There's no charge and no obligation.

https://books2read.com/r/B-A-LRXL-KEKMB

BOOKS 2 READ

Connecting independent readers to independent writers.

www.ingramcontent.com/pod-product-compliance
Lightning Source LLC
Chambersburg PA
CBHW081301040426
42452CB00014B/2594